The Compendium

New Number and Logic Puzzles

How it all began

In May 2000 I had an accident, falling from a ladder, and needed 5 months off work.

Boredom soon set in and as I love numbers I decided to try and devise some number puzzles.

I put three rows of numbers from 1 to 9 on a spreadsheet. I then inserted a formula that added the middle number to the top and bottom numbers and printed out the result.

I then erased all the numbers just leaving the top and bottom totals then by using addition tried to reinstate the correct numbers.

It was then that I had that "Eureka" moment, realising that because the middle row was common to both sums, up and down, it would need logic to place the correct combinations in the right order, and so my ZYGO puzzle was born!

I had a new addictive hobby.

In the years that followed I devised many new number puzzles and compiled computer programs that generated them automatically.

A year or two ago, I thought I would try and get some puzzles published and contacted Andrew Griffin at Tarquin who decided to publish 6 puzzle books for everyone to enjoy.

The Compendium

New Number and Logic Puzzles

Les Page

Tarquin

Publisher's Note

If you have enjoyed this Compendium book and want to get others see the other 5 other books are described opposite - fuller details on www.tarquingroup.com. Enjoy!

Samples of some of the puzzles in other books can be found at the back of this book.

Les Page has asserted his right to be identified as the author of this work under the Copyright, Designs and Patents Act 1988.

© Les Page 2020

ISBN UK (Book) 978-1-913565-06-0

ISBN (EBook) 978-1-913565-07-7

Designed and Printed in the UK

Tarquin

Suite 74, 17 Holywell Hill

St Albans AL1 1DT

UK

www.tarquingroup.com

The Compendium
Contents

Puzzles 1–25

Start on page 1 overleaf. Solutions to each are on reverse side of the puzzle page.

Emojis - tougher puzzles
Book ISBN 9781913565008
Ebook ISBN 9781913565015

Solitary Sudoku
Book ISBN 9781913565046
Ebook ISBN 9781913565053

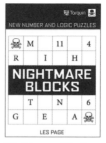

Nightmare Blocks
Book ISBN 9781913565022
Ebook ISBN 9781913565039

And the Starter Books

Nightmare Blocks -
The Starter Book
Book ISBN 9781913565022
Ebook ISBN 9781913565039

Emojis - The Starter Book
Book ISBN 9781913565084
Ebook ISBN 9781913565091

BRAINBOX

PUZZLE 1

USE YOUR " GREY MATTER " TO SOLVE THIS PUZZLE !

?	A	B	?
THIS	×	+	TOTAL
12			56
11			102
10			19
9			23
8			87
7			52
6			20
5			61
4			32
3			37
2			22
1			18

A	B
×	+
1	1
2	2
3	3
4	4
5	5
6	6
7	7
8	8
9	9
10	10
11	11
12	12

Numbers in A & B can only be used once.

Cross off numbers in A & B once placed. Not sure? See the example below!

DO NOT

JUMP TO ☠

CONCLUSIONS!

☹

YOU HAVE

BEEN WARNED !

Example:

THIS	×	A	+	B	=	TOTAL
12	×	2	+	1	=	25

In the example you would cross off 2 in A & 1 in B.

Solution Overleaf

© Les Page 2020   ISBN 9781913565040

For more www.tarquingroup.com

BRAINBOX

SOLUTION 1

☝ GOT IT RIGHT !

☺	A	B	=
THIS	×	+	TOTAL
12	4	8	56
11	9	3	102
10	1	9	19
9	2	5	23
8	10	7	87
7	6	10	52
6	3	2	20
5	12	1	61
4	5	12	32
3	11	4	37
2	8	6	22
1	7	11	28

© Les Page 2020   ISBN 9781913565040   For more www.tarquingroup.com

THE WAREHOUSE

PUZZLE 2

WHAT'S IN STORE HERE ?

A warehouse has 25 large rooms. Each room has six storage areas numbered from 1 to 6. Each room has interlinking glass doors to other rooms. The storage areas adjacent to the interlinking glass doors have the same storage area number as shown in the example below:

6	or	4	4

6	↖ ↗

interlinking glass doors

Insert the missing storage area numbers so that each room contains storage area numbers 1 to 6.

3	5	1
1	5	2
4	3	6
5	3	2

Main grid:

c1	c2	c3	c4	c5	c6	c7	c8	c9
			4	5				
2	1		3	2	6		2	
			5			4		1
5								2
1		2				5		1
4								3
5		1				2		1
3								4
6			4		1			2
2								5
4		6			3			1
6			2					6
3		1				5		3
5								5
1		3			1			4
3				2				3
5			1		4		2	
			5	3				

Solution Overleaf

© Les Page 2020   ISBN 9781913565040

For more www.tarquingroup.com

THE WAREHOUSE

SOLUTION 2

LOOK ! ↘ EVERY ROOM HAS STORAGE AREA NUMBERS 1 TO 6.   👆 ☺

			4	5	1			
2	1	3	3	2	6	6	2	5
6	4	5	5	2	4	4	3	1
5	4	3	3	1	6	6	3	2
1	6	2	2	1	5	5	4	1
4	6	3	3	4	6	6	4	3
5	2	1	1	4	2	2	5	1
3	2	5	5	6	3	3	5	4
6	1	4	4	6	1	1	6	2
2	1	3	3	5	2	2	6	5
4	5	6	6	5	3	3	4	1
6	5	2	2	4	1	1	4	6
3	4	1	1	4	5	5	2	3
5	4	2	2	6	3	3	2	5
1	6	3	3	6	1	1	6	4
3	6	4	4	2	5	5	6	3
5	2	1	1	2	4	4	2	1
			5	3	6			

For more www.tarquingroup.com

PUZZLE 3

THE TWO - WAY MULTIPLICATION PUZZLE.

A × B = ↓				B × C = ↓	Numbers in columns A, B & C on the right must be put in the puzzle so that A × B = the totals on the left & B × C equal the totals on the right.	For each column, cross out numbers as you enter - note they are not in order. ↓ ↓ ↓		
↓	A	B	C	↓	Scribble area	A	B	C
24				16		1	1	1
45				15		3	1	1
7				2		3	2	1
4				20		5	3	2
49				63		6	3	2
42				6		7	4	3
30				42		7	5	3
72				36		7	5	3
27				9		7	6	4
54				18		8	6	5
18				24		8	6	7
3				1		9	7	8
14				16		9	8	8
40				5		9	9	9

Solution Overleaf

 ISBN 9781913565040   For more www.tarquingroup.com

SOLUTION 3

A				B
×		↓		×
B		👍		C
=		☺		=
↓				↓
↓	A	B	C	↓
24	3	8	2	16
45	9	5	3	15
7	7	1	2	2
4	1	4	5	20
49	7	7	9	63
42	7	6	1	6
30	5	6	7	42
72	8	9	4	36
27	9	3	3	9
54	9	6	3	18
18	6	3	8	24
3	3	1	1	1
14	7	2	8	16
40	8	5	1	5

   For more www.tarquingroup.com

PUZZLE 4

YOU WILL NEVER ESCAPE " DOING TIME " ON THIS PUZZLE !

Every block MUST contain 1, 2, 3 & 4 in the left hand column and 1 to 32 MUST be placed in the centre columns to agree the totals.

Cross out numerical values when placed

1	2	3
4	5	6
7	8	9
10	11	12
13	14	15
16	17	18
19	20	21
22	23	24
25	26	27
28	29	30
31	32	☺

Block 1

4	+		=	36
	+		=	20
	+		=	26
2	+		=	12

Block 2

4	+		=	16
	+		=	19
	+		=	9
	+		=	3

Block 3

2	+		=	31
	+		=	4
	+		=	10
	+		=	12

Block 4

3	+		=	18
	+		=	9
	+		=	15
2	+		=	29

Block 5

4	+		=	25
	+		=	5
2	+		=	19
	+		=	28

Block 6

3	+		=	25
	+		=	22
	+		=	35
	+		=	15

Block 7

4	+		=	30
	+		=	26
	+		=	8
	+		=	2

Block 8

1	+		=	19
	+		=	16
4	+		=	34
	+		=	30

Solution Overleaf

© Les Page 2020   ISBN 9781913565040   For more www.tarquingroup.com

SOLUTION 4

LOOK ! ↘ HAVING "DONE TIME" PROVES IT CAN BE SOLVED ! 👌 ☺

4	+	32	=	36
1	+	19	=	20
3	+	23	=	26
2	+	10	=	12

4	+	12	=	16
3	+	16	=	19
2	+	7	=	9
1	+	2	=	3

2	+	29	=	31
1	+	3	=	4
4	+	6	=	10
3	+	9	=	12

3	+	15	=	18
1	+	8	=	9
4	+	11	=	15
2	+	27	=	29

4	+	21	=	25
1	+	4	=	5
2	+	17	=	19
3	+	25	=	28

3	+	22	=	25
2	+	20	=	22
4	+	31	=	35
1	+	14	=	15

4	+	26	=	30
2	+	24	=	26
3	+	5	=	8
1	+	1	=	2

1	+	18	=	19
3	+	13	=	16
4	+	30	=	34
2	+	28	=	30

© Les Page 2020   ISBN 9781913565040   For more www.tarquingroup.com

PUZZLE 5

AT FIRST GLANCE IT MAY LOOK IMPOSSIBLE TO DO! ☹
BUT USING YOUR INITATIVE IT CAN BE DONE! NEVER GIVE UP. ✒

PLACE THESE 33 NUMBERS CORRECTLY TO SOLVE THIS PUZZLE

6	8	15	15	17	20	21	23	27	28	31
32	37	39	40	44	49	51	54	56	60	62
65	67	91	99	104	106	114	118	140	203	254

Just plus... that's all you've got to do!

11	+	☐	=	☐	+	☐	=	☐	+	5	=	☐
+		+		+		+		+		+		+
4	+	16	=	☐	+	☐	=	☐	+	☐	=	☐
=		=		=		=		=		=		=
☐	+	22	=	☐	+	☐	=	☐	+	36	=	☐
+		+		+		+		+		+		+
☐	+	☐	=	60	+	☐	=	☐	+	☐	=	☐
=		=		=		=		=		=		=
43	+	☐	=	97	+	☐	=	☐	+	☐	=	☐
+		+		+		+		+		+		+
13	+	☐	=	21	+	☐	=	42	+	☐	=	☐
=		=		=		=		=		=		=
☐	+	☐	=	☐	+	127	=	245	+	74	=	319

Solution Overleaf

© Les Page 2020   ISBN 9781913565040   For more www.tarquingroup.com

SOLUTION 5

INITATIVE USED.

IT CAN BE DONE !

✦

☺

EVERYTHING ADDED = THE TOTALS !

11	+	6	=	17	+	27	=	44	+	5	=	49
+		+		+		+		+		+		+
4	+	16	=	20	+	40	=	60	+	31	=	91
=		=		=		=		=		=		=
15	+	22	=	37	+	67	=	104	+	36	=	140
+		+		+		+		+		+		+
28	+	32	=	60	+	39	=	99	+	15	=	114
=		=		=		=		=		=		=
43	+	54	=	97	+	106	=	203	+	51	=	254
+		+		+		+		+		+		+
13	+	8	=	21	+	21	=	42	+	23	=	65
=		=		=		=		=		=		=
56	+	62	=	118	+	127	=	245	+	74	=	319

For more www.tarquingroup.com

PUZZLE 6

USE YOUR " GREY MATTER " TO SOLVE THIS PUZZLE !

?	A	B	?
THIS	×	+	TOTAL
12			53
11			36
10			108
9			47
8			95
7			62
6			40
5			44
4			9
3			39
2			35
1			11

A	B
×	+
1	1
2	2
3	3
4	4
5	5
6	6
7	7
8	8
9	9
10	10
11	11
12	12

Numbers in A & B can only be used once.

Cross off numbers in A & B once placed. Not sure? See the example below!

DO NOT

JUMP TO ☠

CONCLUSIONS!

☹

YOU HAVE

BEEN WARNED !

Example:

THIS	×	A	+	B	=	TOTAL
12	×	2	+	1	=	25

In the example you would cross off 2 in A & 1 in B.

Solution Overleaf

© Les Page 2020   ISBN 9781913565040

For more www.tarquingroup.com

BRAINBOX

SOLUTION 6

☝ GOT IT RIGHT !

☺	A	B	=
THIS	×	+	TOTAL
12	4	5	53
11	3	3	36
10	10	8	108
9	5	2	47
8	11	7	95
7	8	6	62
6	6	4	40
5	7	9	44
4	2	1	9
3	9	12	39
2	12	11	35
1	1	10	11

© Les Page 2020   ISBN 9781913565040   For more www.tarquingroup.com

THE WAREHOUSE

PUZZLE 7

WHAT'S IN STORE HERE ?

A warehouse has 25 large rooms. Each room has six storage areas numbered from 1 to 6. Each room has interlinking glass doors to other rooms. The storage areas adjacent to the interlinking glass doors have the same storage area number as shown in the example below:

6	or	4	4
6			

interlinking glass doors

Insert the missing storage area numbers so that each room contains storage area numbers 1 to 6.

3	5	1
1	5	2
4	3	6
5	3	2

			1	4			
	5	2			6		4
6		4		3		1	5
4							3
5		3				4	5
1							2
4		5			3		5
2							1
6			1		5		3
3							4
1			6		2		5
6			3				6
2			5			4	2
4							4
5			2			5	1
2				3			2
4		5				1	3
			4	2			

Solution Overleaf

For more www.tarquingroup.com

SOLUTION 7

LOOK ! ↘ EVERY ROOM HAS STORAGE AREA NUMBERS 1 TO 6. 👌 ☺

			1	4	5			
3	5	2	2	3	6	6	3	4
6	1	4	4	3	1	1	2	5
4	1	2	2	5	6	6	2	3
5	6	3	3	5	4	4	1	5
1	6	2	2	1	6	6	1	2
4	3	5	5	1	3	3	4	5
2	3	4	4	6	2	2	4	1
6	5	1	1	6	5	5	6	3
3	5	2	2	4	3	3	6	4
1	4	6	6	4	2	2	1	5
6	4	3	3	1	5	5	1	6
2	1	5	5	1	4	4	3	2
4	1	3	3	6	2	2	3	4
5	6	2	2	6	5	5	6	1
2	6	1	1	3	4	4	6	2
4	3	5	5	3	1	1	3	5
			4	2	6			

PUZZLE 8

THE TWO - WAY MULTIPLICATION PUZZLE.

A × B = ↓				B × C = ↓	Numbers in columns A, B & C on the right must be put in the puzzle so that A × B = the totals on the left & B × C equal the totals on the right.	For each column, cross out numbers as you enter - note they are not in order. ↓ ↓ ↓		
↓	A	B	C	↓	Scribble area	A	B	C
32				40		1	2	1
30				10		1	3	2
24				32		2	4	2
48				48		2	5	3
42				35		2	5	4
4				16		2	5	5
10				45		3	6	5
6				18		3	6	6
72				18		4	6	7
5				5		6	7	7
8				28		6	8	8
18				54		6	8	8
12				42		7	8	9
21				24		8	9	9

Solution Overleaf

© Les Page 2020   ISBN 9781913565040   For more www.tarquingroup.com

SOLUTION 8

A				B
×		↓		×
B		👍		C
=		☺		=
↓				↓
↓	A	B	C	↓
32	4	8	5	40
30	6	5	2	10
24	3	8	4	32
48	6	8	6	48
42	6	7	5	35
4	2	2	8	16
10	2	5	9	45
6	1	6	3	18
72	8	9	2	18
5	1	5	1	5
8	2	4	7	28
18	3	6	9	54
12	2	6	7	42
21	7	3	8	24

PUZZLE 9

YOU WILL NEVER ESCAPE " DOING TIME " ON THIS PUZZLE !

Every block MUST contain 1, 2, 3 & 4 in the left hand column and 1 to 32 MUST be placed in the centre columns to agree the totals.

1	+		=	28
	+		=	6
	+		=	14
4	+		=	13

4	+		=	11
	+		=	26
	+		=	15
	+		=	16

2	+		=	10
	+		=	8
	+		=	28
	+		=	11

4	+		=	30
	+		=	19
	+		=	33
2	+		=	16

2	+		=	30
	+		=	21
3	+		=	5
	+		=	15

3	+		=	19
	+		=	2
	+		=	10
	+		=	33

1	+		=	20
	+		=	31
	+		=	24
	+		=	29

1	+		=	18
	+		=	24
4	+		=	8
	+		=	35

Cross out numerical values when placed

1	2	3
4	5	6
7	8	9
10	11	12
13	14	15
16	17	18
19	20	21
22	23	24
25	26	27
28	29	30
31	32	☺

Solution Overleaf

© Les Page 2020   ISBN 9781913565040   For more www.tarquingroup.com

SOLUTION 9

LOOK ! ↘ HAVING "DONE TIME" PROVES IT CAN BE SOLVED ! 👌 ☺

1	+	27	=	28
3	+	3	=	6
2	+	12	=	14
4	+	9	=	13

4	+	7	=	11
3	+	23	=	26
2	+	13	=	15
1	+	15	=	16

2	+	8	=	10
3	+	5	=	8
4	+	24	=	28
1	+	10	=	11

4	+	26	=	30
1	+	18	=	19
3	+	30	=	33
2	+	14	=	16

2	+	28	=	30
1	+	20	=	21
3	+	2	=	5
4	+	11	=	15

3	+	16	=	19
1	+	1	=	2
4	+	6	=	10
2	+	31	=	33

1	+	19	=	20
2	+	29	=	31
3	+	21	=	24
4	+	25	=	29

1	+	17	=	18
2	+	22	=	24
4	+	4	=	8
3	+	32	=	35

© Les Page 2020   ISBN 9781913565040

PUZZLE 10

AT FIRST GLANCE IT MAY LOOK IMPOSSIBLE TO DO. ☹

BUT USING YOUR INITATIVE IT CAN BE DONE. NEVER GIVE UP. ✍

PLACE THESE 33 NUMBERS CORRECTLY TO SOLVE THIS PUZZLE

6	10	11	17	18	25	30	31	34	36	41
42	47	58	64	66	72	75	77	81	87	87
109	116	117	117	122	133	199	226	238	246	310

Just plus... that's all you've got to do!

39 + ☐ = ☐ + ☐ = ☐ + 5 = ☐
+ + + + + + +
☐ + ☐ = ☐ + 24 = 82 + ☐ = ☐
= = = = = = =
56 + ☐ = ☐ + ☐ = ☐ + 39 = ☐
+ + + + + + +
☐ + ☐ = 41 + ☐ = ☐ + ☐ = ☐
= = = = = = =
☐ + ☐ = 174 + 72 = ☐ + ☐ = ☐
+ + + + + + +
22 + ☐ = 52 + ☐ = 70 + ☐ = ☐
= = = = = = =
☐ + ☐ = ☐ + 90 = 316 + 75 = 391

Solution Overleaf

For more www.tarquingroup.com

JUST PLUS

SOLUTION 10

INITATIVE USED.
IT CAN BE DONE !
👌
☺
EVERYTHING ADDED = THE TOTALS !

39	+	36	=	75	+	42	=	117	+	5	=	122

39	+	36	=	75	+	42	=	117	+	5	=	122
+		+		+		+		+		+
17	+	41	=	58	+	24	=	82	+	34	=	116
=		=		=		=		=		=
56	+	77	=	133| +	66	=	199| +	39	=	238
+		+		+		+		+		+
31	+	10	=	41	+	6	=	47	+	25	=	72
=		=		=		=		=		=
87	+	87	=	174| +	72	=	246| +	64	=	310
+		+		+		+		+		+
22	+	30	=	52	+	18	=	70	+	11	=	81
=		=		=		=		=		=
109	+	117	=	226	+	90	=	316	+	75	=	391

BRAINBOX

PUZZLE 11
USE YOUR " GREY MATTER " TO SOLVE THIS PUZZLE !

?	A	B	?
THIS	×	+	TOTAL
12			27
11			122
10			55
9			90
8			72
7			83
6			37
5			42
4			16
3			13
2			19
1			14

A	B
×	+
1	1
2	2
3	3
4	4
5	5
6	6
7	7
8	8
9	9
10	10
11	11
12	12

Numbers in A & B can only be used once.

Cross off numbers in A & B once placed. Not sure? See the example below!

DO NOT

JUMP TO ☠

CONCLUSIONS!

☹

YOU HAVE

BEEN WARNED !

Example:

THIS	×	A	+	B	=	TOTAL
12	×	2	+	1	=	25

In the example you would cross off 2 in A & 1 in B.

Solution Overleaf

© Les Page 2020   ISBN 9781913565040   For more www.tarquingroup.com

BRAINBOX

SOLUTION 11

👍 GOT IT RIGHT !

☺	A	B	=
THIS	×	+	TOTAL
12	2	3	27
11	10	12	122
10	5	5	55
9	9	9	90
8	8	8	72
7	11	6	83
6	6	1	37
5	7	7	42
4	3	4	16
3	1	10	13
2	4	11	19
1	12	2	14

For more www.tarquingroup.com

THE WAREHOUSE

PUZZLE 12

WHAT'S IN STORE HERE ?

A warehouse has 25 large rooms. Each room has six storage areas numbered from 1 to 6. Each room has interlinking glass doors to other rooms. The storage areas adjacent to the interlinking glass doors have the same storage area number as shown in the example below:

6	or	4	4
6	↖ ↗		

interlinking glass doors

Insert the missing storage area numbers so that each room contains storage area numbers 1 to 6.

3	5	1
1	5	2
4	3	6
5	3	2

Main grid:

			2	6				
4	5	1			3		4	
		6		4	2			5
6								4
5			4		6			5
2								1
6		5				4		5
1								2
3		2				5		4
4								6
2		3			1			5
3			4					3
1		5			6			1
6								6
5			1		5			2
1								1
6		5		4	2		4	
			6	1				

Solution Overleaf

For more www.tarquingroup.com

SOLUTION 12

LOOK ! ↘ HAVING "DONE TIME" PROVES IT CAN BE SOLVED ! ♠ ☺

			2	6	5			
4	5	1	1	4	3	3	4	6
3	2	6	6	4	2	2	1	5
6	2	1	1	5	3	3	1	4
5	3	4	4	5	6	6	2	5
2	3	1	1	2	3	3	2	1
6	4	5	5	2	4	4	6	5
1	4	6	6	3	1	1	6	2
3	5	2	2	3	5	5	3	4
4	5	1	1	6	4	4	3	6
2	6	3	3	6	1	1	2	5
3	6	4	4	2	5	5	2	3
1	2	5	5	2	6	6	4	1
6	2	4	4	3	1	1	4	6
5	3	1	1	3	5	5	3	2
1	3	2	2	4	6	6	3	1
6	4	5	5	4	2	2	4	5
			6	1	3			

   For more www.tarquingroup.com

PUZZLE 13

THE TWO - WAY MULTIPLICATION PUZZLE.

A × B = ↓				B × C = ↓	Numbers in columns A, B & C on the right must be put in the puzzle so that A × B = the totals on the left & B × C equal the totals on the right.	For each column, cross out numbers as you enter - note they are not in order. ↓ ↓ ↓		
↓	A	B	C	↓	Scribble area	A	B	C
18				3		1	1	1
4				3		2	3	1
10				40		2	3	1
30				20		3	3	1
28				20		4	3	2
21				24		4	3	3
54				30		6	4	4
49				7		6	4	5
3				6		7	5	5
12				54		7	5	8
24				3		7	6	8
36				36		8	6	8
9				24		9	7	9
32				8		9	8	9

Solution Overleaf

© Les Page 2020   ISBN 9781913565040   For more www.tarquingroup.com

SOLUTION 13

A				B
×		↓		×
B		👍		C
=		☺		=
↓				↓
↓	A	B	C	↓
18	6	3	1	3
4	4	1	3	3
10	2	5	8	40
30	6	5	4	20
28	7	4	5	20
21	7	3	8	24
54	9	6	5	30
49	7	7	1	7
3	1	3	2	6
12	2	6	9	54
24	8	3	1	3
36	9	4	9	36
9	3	3	8	24
32	4	8	1	8

ALCATRAZ

PUZZLE 14

YOU WILL NEVER ESCAPE " DOING TIME " ON THIS PUZZLE !

Every block MUST contain 1, 2, 3 & 4 in the left hand column and 1 to 32 MUST be placed in the centre columns to agree the totals.

4	+		=	25
	+		=	12
	+		=	27
2	+		=	19

4	+		=	31
	+		=	10
	+		=	20
	+		=	15

2	+		=	18
	+		=	31
	+		=	27
	+		=	15

1	+		=	7
	+		=	9
	+		=	31
3	+		=	5

4	+		=	19
	+		=	28
1	+		=	23
	+		=	34

1	+		=	26
	+		=	32
	+		=	7
	+		=	12

4	+		=	7
	+		=	11
	+		=	23
	+		=	20

3	+		=	35
	+		=	10
4	+		=	17
	+		=	2

Cross out numerical values when placed

1	2	3
4	5	6
7	8	9
10	11	12
13	14	15
16	17	18
19	20	21
22	23	24
25	26	27
28	29	30
31	32	☺

Solution Overleaf

For more www.tarquingroup.com

SOLUTION 14

LOOK ! ↘ HAVING "DONE TIME" PROVES IT CAN BE SOLVED ! ✎ ☺

4	+	21	=	25
1	+	11	=	12
3	+	24	=	27
2	+	17	=	19

4	+	27	=	31
3	+	7	=	10
2	+	18	=	20
1	+	14	=	15

2	+	16	=	18
1	+	30	=	31
4	+	23	=	27
3	+	12	=	15

1	+	6	=	7
4	+	5	=	9
2	+	29	=	31
3	+	2	=	5

4	+	15	=	19
2	+	26	=	28
1	+	22	=	23
3	+	31	=	34

1	+	25	=	26
4	+	28	=	32
3	+	4	=	7
2	+	10	=	12

4	+	3	=	7
2	+	9	=	11
3	+	20	=	23
1	+	19	=	20

3	+	32	=	35
2	+	8	=	10
4	+	13	=	17
1	+	1	=	2

   For more www.tarquingroup.com

JUST PLUS

PUZZLE 15

AT FIRST GLANCE IT MAY LOOK IMPOSSIBLE TO DO! ☹
BUT USING YOUR INITATIVE IT CAN BE DONE! NEVER GIVE UP. ✎

PLACE THESE 33 NUMBERS CORRECTLY TO SOLVE THIS PUZZLE

5	7	12	14	16	20	20	24	29	38	40
43	48	52	54	63	63	66	66	74	74	78
78	98	98	102	112	122	125	168	200	266	274

Just plus... that's all you've got to do!

6	+ ☐ = ☐	+ ☐ = ☐	+ 39 = ☐
+	+	+	+

The puzzle grid (addition cross-grid):

- Row 1: **6** + ☐ = ☐ + ☐ = ☐ + **39** = ☐
- Row 2: ☐ + **38** = ☐ + ☐ = **59** + ☐ = ☐
- Row 3: **22** + ☐ = ☐ + ☐ = ☐ + **46** = ☐
- Row 4: ☐ + **26** = ☐ + ☐ = ☐ + ☐ = ☐
- Row 5: **34** + ☐ = ☐ + **88** = ☐ + ☐ = ☐
- Row 6: ☐ + **8** = **37** + **37** = ☐ + ☐ = ☐
- Row 7: ☐ + **86** = **149** + ☐ = ☐ + **90** = **364**

(All vertical connections between rows are "+", and every row/column resolves with "=".)

Solution Overleaf

ISBN 9781913565040   For more www.tarquingroup.com

SOLUTION 15

INITATIVE USED.

IT CAN BE DONE !

👌

☺

EVERYTHING ADDED = THE TOTALS !

6	+	14	=	20	+	43	=	63	+	39	=	102
+		+		+		+		+		+		+
16	+	38	=	54	+	5	=	59	+	7	=	66
=		=		=		=		=		=		=
22	+	52	=	74	+	48	=	122	+	46	=	168
+		+		+		+		+		+		+
12	+	26	=	38	+	40	=	78	+	20	=	98
=		=		=		=		=		=		=
34	+	78	=	112	+	88	=	200	+	66	=	266
+		+		+		+		+		+		+
29	+	8	=	37	+	37	=	74	+	24	=	98
=		=		=		=		=		=		=
63	+	86	=	149	+	125	=	274	+	90	=	364

BRAINBOX

PUZZLE 16

USE YOUR " GREY MATTER " TO SOLVE THIS PUZZLE !

?	A	B	?
THIS	×	+	TOTAL
12			24
11			134
10			41
9			57
8			44
7			80
6			48
5			28
4			43
3			33
2			5
1			16

A	B
×	+
1	1
2	2
3	3
4	4
5	5
6	6
7	7
8	8
9	9
10	10
11	11
12	12

Numbers in A & B can only be used once.

Cross off numbers in A & B once placed. Not sure? See the example below!

DO NOT

JUMP TO ☠

CONCLUSIONS!

☹

YOU HAVE

BEEN WARNED !

Example:

THIS	×	A	+	B	=	TOTAL
12	×	2	+	1	=	25

In the example you would cross off 2 in A & 1 in B.

Solution Overleaf

© Les Page 2020   ISBN 9781913565040   For more www.tarquingroup.com

BRAINBOX

SOLUTION 16

✋ GOT IT RIGHT !

☺	A	B	=
THIS	×	+	TOTAL
12	1	12	24
11	12	2	134
10	3	11	41
9	6	3	57
8	5	4	44
7	10	10	80
6	7	6	48
5	4	8	28
4	9	7	43
3	8	9	33
2	2	1	5
1	11	5	16

THE WAREHOUSE

PUZZLE 17
WHAT'S IN STORE HERE ?

A warehouse has 25 large rooms. Each room has six storage areas numbered from 1 to 6. Each room has interlinking glass doors to other rooms. The storage areas adjacent to the interlinking glass doors have the same storage area number as shown in the example below:

6	or	4	4
6	↖ ↗		

interlinking glass doors

Insert the missing storage area numbers so that each room contains storage area numbers 1 to 6.

3	5	1
1	5	2
4	3	6
5	3	2

			1	4			
6		2			3		1
3			1	6	5		4
1							6
4		6			1		4
5							2
1			4		6		4
2							5
3			5			4	6
6							1
5			3		2		4
3			6				3
2		4			1		2
1							1
4		2				4	5
2							2
1			4	6	5		4
			1	2			

Solution Overleaf

© Les Page 2020   ISBN 9781913565040   For more www.tarquingroup.com

THE WAREHOUSE

SOLUTION 17

LOOK ! ↘ HAVING "DONE TIME" PROVES IT CAN BE SOLVED ! ♠ ☺

			5	1	4			
6	4	2	2	6	3	3	6	1
3	5	1	1	6	5	5	2	4
1	5	2	2	4	3	3	2	6
4	3	6	6	4	1	1	5	4
5	3	2	2	5	3	3	5	2
1	6	4	4	5	6	6	1	4
2	6	1	1	3	2	2	1	5
3	4	5	5	3	4	4	3	6
6	4	2	2	1	6	6	3	1
5	1	3	3	1	2	2	5	4
3	1	6	6	5	4	4	5	3
2	5	4	4	5	1	1	6	2
1	5	6	6	3	2	2	6	1
4	3	2	2	3	4	4	3	5
2	3	5	5	6	1	1	3	2
1	6	4	4	6	5	5	6	4
			1	2	3			

For more www.tarquingroup.com

MULTI-TASKING

PUZZLE 18

THE TWO - WAY MULTIPLICATION PUZZLE.

A × B = ↓	A	B	C	B × C = ↓	Scribble area	A ↓	B ↓	C ↓
					Numbers in columns A, B & C on the right must be put in the puzzle so that A × B = the totals on the left & B × C equal the totals on the right.	For each column, cross out numbers as you enter - note they are not in order.		
40				72		1	1	1
8				6		2	3	1
72				63		3	4	2
24				18		4	5	6
16				72		5	5	6
20				40		5	6	6
54				9		6	6	6
25				30		6	8	6
36				6		7	8	7
9				54		7	8	7
32				24		8	9	8
56				56		8	9	9
27				18		8	9	9
42				54		8	9	9

Solution Overleaf

 ISBN 9781913565040   For more www.tarquingroup.com

SOLUTION 18

A				B
×		↓		×
B		👍		C
=		☺		=
↓				↓
↓	A	B	C	↓
40	5	8	9	72
8	8	1	6	6
72	8	9	7	63
24	8	3	6	18
16	2	8	9	72
20	4	5	8	40
54	6	9	1	9
25	5	5	6	30
36	6	6	1	6
9	1	9	6	54
32	8	4	6	24
56	7	8	7	56
27	3	9	2	18
42	7	6	9	54

© Les Page 2020   ISBN 9781913565040

ALCATRAZ

PUZZLE 19

YOU WILL NEVER ESCAPE " DOING TIME " ON THIS PUZZLE !

Every block MUST contain 1, 2, 3 & 4 in the left hand column and 1 to 32 MUST be placed in the centre columns to agree the totals.

1	2	3
4	5	6
7	8	9
10	11	12
13	14	15
16	17	18
19	20	21
22	23	24
25	26	27
28	29	30
31	32	☺

Cross out numerical values when placed

Block 1

3	+		=	9
	+		=	34
	+		=	10
4	+		=	17

Block 2

2	+		=	24
	+		=	8
	+		=	22
	+		=	18

Block 3

4	+		=	15
	+		=	2
	+		=	22
	+		=	20

Block 4

1	+		=	26
	+		=	33
	+		=	19
4	+		=	7

Block 5

4	+		=	27
	+		=	5
2	+		=	30
	+		=	28

Block 6

4	+		=	30
	+		=	6
	+		=	11
	+		=	33

Block 7

3	+		=	8
	+		=	23
	+		=	28
	+		=	16

Block 8

2	+		=	31
	+		=	19
4	+		=	12
	+		=	15

Solution Overleaf

© Les Page 2020   ISBN 9781913565040

For more www.tarquingroup.com

ALCATRAZ

SOLUTION 19

LOOK ! ↘ HAVING "DONE TIME" PROVES IT CAN BE SOLVED ! ✆ ☺

3	+	6	=	9
2	+	32	=	34
1	+	9	=	10
4	+	13	=	17

2	+	22	=	24
1	+	7	=	8
3	+	19	=	22
4	+	14	=	18

4	+	11	=	15
1	+	1	=	2
2	+	20	=	22
3	+	17	=	20

1	+	25	=	26
2	+	31	=	33
3	+	16	=	19
4	+	3	=	7

4	+	23	=	27
3	+	2	=	5
2	+	28	=	30
1	+	27	=	28

4	+	26	=	30
2	+	4	=	6
1	+	10	=	11
3	+	30	=	33

3	+	5	=	8
2	+	21	=	23
4	+	24	=	28
1	+	15	=	16

2	+	29	=	31
1	+	18	=	19
4	+	8	=	12
3	+	12	=	15

For more www.tarquingroup.com

PUZZLE 20

AT FIRST GLANCE IT MAY LOOK IMPOSSIBLE TO DO! ☹
BUT USING YOUR INITATIVE IT CAN BE DONE! NEVER GIVE UP. ✎

PLACE THESE 33 NUMBERS CORRECTLY TO SOLVE THIS PUZZLE

3	10	11	15	23	24	26	27	28	28	29
32	33	36	41	44	50	59	64	81	84	88
90	93	95	95	112	116	122	139	202	211	261

Just plus... that's all you've got to do!

14	+		=		+		=		+	12	=	
+		+		+		+		+		+		+
	+		=	59	+	25	=		+		=	
=		=		=		=		=		=		=
40	+	48	=		+		=		+		=	
+		+		+		+		+		+		+
	+	18	=		+		=		+		=	
=		=		=		=		=		=		=
	+	66	=	147	+		=		+		=	
+		+		+		+		+		+		+
31	+		=	55	+		=	65	+		=	
=		=		=		=		=		=		=
	+		=		+	74	=	276	+	78	=	354

Solution Overleaf

© Les Page 2020   ISBN 9781913565040   For more www.tarquingroup.com

JUST PLUS

SOLUTION 20

INITATIVE USED.

IT CAN BE DONE !

☀

☺

EVERYTHING ADDED = THE TOTALS !

14	+	15	=	29	+	3	=	32	+	12	=	44

14	+	15	=	29	+	3	=	32	+	12	=	44
+		+		+		+		+		+		+
26	+	33	=	59	+	25	=	84	+	11	=	95
=		=		=		=		=		=		=
40	+	48	=	88	+	28	=	116	+	23	=	139
+		+		+		+		+		+		+
41	+	18	=	59	+	36	=	95	+	27	=	122
=		=		=		=		=		=		=
81	+	66	=	147	+	64	=	211	+	50	=	261
+		+		+		+		+		+		+
31	+	24	=	55	+	10	=	65	+	28	=	93
=		=		=		=		=		=		=
112	+	90	=	202	+	74	=	276	+	78	=	354

For more www.tarquingroup.com

BRAINBOX

PUZZLE 21

USE YOUR " GREY MATTER " TO SOLVE THIS PUZZLE !

?	A	B	?
THIS	×	+	TOTAL
12			21
11			69
10			126
9			53
8			27
7			31
6			36
5			47
4			48
3			22
2			23
1			12

A	B
×	+
1	1
2	2
3	3
4	4
5	5
6	6
7	7
8	8
9	9
10	10
11	11
12	12

Numbers in A & B can only be used once.

Cross off numbers in A & B once placed. Not sure? See the example below!

DO NOT

JUMP TO ☠

CONCLUSIONS!

☹

YOU HAVE

BEEN WARNED !

Example:

THIS	×	A	+	B	=	TOTAL
12	×	2	+	1	=	25

In the example you would cross off 2 in A & 1 in B.

Solution Overleaf

For more www.tarquingroup.com

BRAINBOX

SOLUTION 21

👍 GOT IT RIGHT !

☺	A	B	=
THIS	×	+	TOTAL
12	1	9	21
11	6	3	69
10	12	6	126
9	5	8	53
8	2	11	27
7	3	10	31
6	4	12	36
5	8	7	47
4	11	4	48
3	7	1	22
2	9	5	23
1	10	2	12

THE WAREHOUSE

PUZZLE 22

WHAT'S IN STORE HERE ?

A warehouse has 25 large rooms. Each room has six storage areas numbered from 1 to 6. Each room has interlinking glass doors to other rooms. The storage areas adjacent to the interlinking glass doors have the same storage area number as shown in the example below:

6	or	4	4
6	↖ ↗		

interlinking
glass doors

Insert the missing storage area numbers so that each room contains storage area numbers 1 to 6.

3	5	1
1	5	2
4	3	6
5	3	2

				5	1			
4	1	3				6	4	
		5		4	2			1
5								4
1			4			5		1
2								3
5		1			4			1
3								2
6		2				1		4
4								5
2		6			3			1
6			4					6
3			1		5			3
5								5
1			3			1		2
								3
5	4		1	4		2	4	
				3	6			

Solution Overleaf

                    For more www.tarquingroup.com

SOLUTION 22

LOOK ! ↘ HAVING "DONE TIME" PROVES IT CAN BE SOLVED ! ♠ ☺

			2	5	1			
4	1	3	3	4	6	6	4	5
6	2	5	5	4	2	2	3	1
5	2	3	3	1	6	6	3	4
1	6	4	4	1	5	5	2	1
2	6	3	3	2	6	6	2	3
5	4	1	1	2	4	4	5	1
3	4	5	5	6	3	3	5	2
6	1	2	2	6	1	1	6	4
4	1	3	3	5	4	4	6	5
2	5	6	6	5	3	3	2	1
6	5	4	4	2	1	1	2	6
3	2	1	1	2	5	5	4	3
5	2	4	4	6	3	3	4	5
1	6	3	3	6	1	1	6	2
3	6	2	2	4	5	5	6	3
5	4	1	1	4	2	2	4	1
			5	3	6			

     For more www.tarquingroup.com

PUZZLE 23

THE TWO - WAY MULTIPLICATION PUZZLE.

A × B = ↓				B × C = ↓	Numbers in columns A, B & C on the right must be put in the puzzle so that A × B = the totals on the left & B × C equal the totals on the right.	For each column, cross out numbers as you enter - note they are not in order. ↓ ↓ ↓		
↓	A	B	C	↓	Scribble area	A	B	C
21				3		1	1	1
6				1		2	1	1
9				18		4	1	1
5				2		4	1	2
20				24		5	2	2
8				8		5	3	2
4				2		6	4	4
42				35		6	4	4
18				9		7	5	4
16				16		7	7	5
28				16		7	7	6
45				20		8	8	7
32				32		8	9	8
49				49		9	9	8

Solution Overleaf

For more www.tarquingroup.com

SOLUTION 23

A			B
×	↓		×
B	👍		C
=	☺		=
↓			↓

↓	A	B	C	↓
21	7	3	1	3
6	6	1	1	1
9	1	9	2	18
5	5	1	2	2
20	5	4	6	24
8	8	1	8	8
4	4	1	2	2
42	6	7	5	35
18	2	9	1	9
16	8	2	8	16
28	7	4	4	16
45	9	5	4	20
32	4	8	4	32
49	7	7	7	49

© Les Page 2020   ISBN 9781913565040

PUZZLE 24

YOU WILL NEVER ESCAPE " DOING TIME " ON THIS PUZZLE !

Every block MUST contain 1, 2, 3 & 4 in the left hand column and 1 to 32 MUST be placed in the centre columns to agree the totals.

Cross out numerical values when placed

1	2	3
4	5	6
7	8	9
10	11	12
13	14	15
16	17	18
19	20	21
22	23	24
25	26	27
28	29	30
31	32	☺

Block 1

2	+		=	13
	+		=	20
	+		=	11
3	+		=	18

Block 2

1	+		=	17
	+		=	28
	+		=	32
	+		=	31

Block 3

3	+		=	7
	+		=	9
	+		=	23
	+		=	10

Block 4

1	+		=	18
	+		=	6
	+		=	12
3	+		=	28

Block 5

4	+		=	36
	+		=	11
1	+		=	21
	+		=	3

Block 6

3	+		=	21
	+		=	16
	+		=	25
	+		=	10

Block 7

3	+		=	33
	+		=	32
	+		=	26
	+		=	25

Block 8

1	+		=	13
	+		=	7
3	+		=	16
	+		=	30

Solution Overleaf

© Les Page 2020   ISBN 9781913565040   For more www.tarquingroup.com

ALCATRAZ

SOLUTION 24

LOOK ! ↘ HAVING "DONE TIME" PROVES IT CAN BE SOLVED ! ✎ ☺

2	+	11	=	13
1	+	19	=	20
4	+	7	=	11
3	+	15	=	18

1	+	16	=	17
2	+	26	=	28
3	+	29	=	32
4	+	27	=	31

3	+	4	=	7
4	+	5	=	9
2	+	21	=	23
1	+	9	=	10

1	+	17	=	18
4	+	2	=	6
2	+	10	=	12
3	+	25	=	28

4	+	32	=	36
3	+	8	=	11
1	+	20	=	21
2	+	1	=	3

3	+	18	=	21
2	+	14	=	16
1	+	24	=	25
4	+	6	=	10

3	+	30	=	33
1	+	31	=	32
4	+	22	=	26
2	+	23	=	25

1	+	12	=	13
4	+	3	=	7
3	+	13	=	16
2	+	28	=	30

JUST PLUS

PUZZLE 25

AT FIRST GLANCE IT MAY LOOK IMPOSSIBLE TO DO! ☹
BUT USING YOUR INITATIVE IT CAN BE DONE! NEVER GIVE UP. ✎

PLACE THESE 33 NUMBERS CORRECTLY TO SOLVE THIS PUZZLE

3	6	11	19	20	20	28	33	34	35	36
36	39	39	41	55	56	68	70	85	89	106
111	118	121	131	145	174	194	220	230	266	341

Just plus... that's all you've got to do!

30 + ☐ = ☐ + ☐ = ☐ + 34 = ☐
+ + + + + + +
42 + ☐ = ☐ + ☐ = 90 + ☐ = ☐
= = = = = = =
72 + ☐ = ☐ + ☐ = ☐ + 75 = ☐
+ + + + + + +
☐ + ☐ = ☐ + 17 = ☐ + ☐ = ☐
= = = = = = =
107 + 67 = ☐ + ☐ = ☐ + ☐ = ☐
+ + + + + + +
☐ + 9 = ☐ + 16 = 36 + ☐ = ☐
= = = = = = =
☐ + 76 = ☐ + 72 = ☐ + 114 = 380

Solution Overleaf

For more www.tarquingroup.com

SOLUTION 25

INITATIVE USED.

IT CAN BE DONE !

☙

☺

EVERYTHING ADDED = THE TOTALS !

30	+	6	=	36	+	19	=	55	+	34	=	89
+		+		+		+		+		+		+
42	+	28	=	70	+	20	=	90	+	41	=	131
=		=		=		=		=		=		=
72	+	34	=	106	+	39	=	145	+	75	=	220
+		+		+		+		+		+		+
35	+	33	=	68	+	17	=	85	+	36	=	121
=		=		=		=		=		=		=
107	+	67	=	174	+	56	=	230	+	111	=	341
+		+		+		+		+		+		+
11	+	9	=	20	+	16	=	36	+	3	=	39
=		=		=		=		=		=		=
118	+	76	=	194	+	72	=	266	+	114	=	380

The 15 letters in **NIGHTMARE BLOCKS** have different numerical values. Place values to agree sum totals horizontally, vertically and diagonally.

Cross out numerical values when placed

↓ = ∩ Enter values when worked out   Green boxes are "given" values

N	=	
I	=	
G	=	18
H	=	19
T	=	
M	=	
A	=	1
R	=	
E	=	
B	=	4
L	=	
O	=	
C	=	
K	=	
S	=	21

↘	↓	↓	↓	↓	↓	↙
→	R	N	H	C	M	51
→	K	A	O	S	E	58
→	R	I	H	T	L	58
→	T	B	B	G	E	55
→	N	M	A	I	G	30
52	58	16	60	75	43	67

↘	↓	↓	↓	↓	↓	↙
→						51
→		1		21		58
→			19			58
→		4		18		55
→						30
52	58	16	60	75	43	67

| 1 |
| 2 |
| 3 |
| 4 |
| 5 |
| 6 |
| 9 |
| 10 |
| 11 |
| 13 |
| 17 |
| 18 |
| 19 |
| 20 |
| 21 |

Solution Overleaf

SOLUTION

↘	↓	↓	↓	↓	↓	↙
→	R	N	H	C	M	51
→	K	A	O	S	E	58
→	R	I	H	T	L	58
→	T	B	B	G	E	55
→	N	M	A	I	G	30
52	58	16	60	75	43	67

↘	↓	↓	↓	↓	↓	↙
→	11	6	19	13	2	51
→	10	1	17	21	9	58
→	11	3	19	20	5	58
→	20	4	4	18	9	55
→	6	2	1	3	18	30
52	58	16	60	75	43	67

A	=	1
M	=	2
I	=	3
B	=	4
L	=	5
N	=	6
E	=	9
K	=	10
R	=	11
C	=	13
O	=	17
G	=	18
H	=	19
T	=	20
S	=	21

PUZZLE PREVIEW EMOJIS

15 EMOJIS have different numerical values. Put the values in the puzzle grid to agree the sum totals horizontally, vertically and diagonally.

↓ = ∩ Enter values when worked out   Yellow boxes are "given" values ✗

🫰	=	20
😐	=	
👉	=	
❖	=	6
✈	=	
🖐	=	
☹	=	
☺	=	
👍	=	
💣	=	16
⌘	=	8
☝	=	
🏳	=	
👎	=	
☠	=	21

Top grid

↘	↓	↓	↓	↓	↓	↙
→	👍	🖐	😐	☹	👎	47
→	😐	⌘	🏳	💣	☝	68
→	✈	💣	❖	👉	☺	55
→	☺	☠	🖐	🫰	☠	90
→	✈	🏳	⌘	❖	☹	40
48	38	72	55	70	65	50

Bottom grid

↘	↓	↓	↓	↓	↓	↙
→						47
→		8		16		68
→			6			55
→		21		20		90
→						40
48	38	72	55	70	65	50

2
3
5
6
8
11
12
13
14
15
16
17
18
20
21

Solution Overleaf

SOLUTION

↘	↓	↓	↓	↓	↓	↙
→	👍	🖐	😐	☹	👎	47
→	😐	⌘	🚩	💣	☝	68
→	✈	💣	❖	👉	☺	55
→	☺	☠	🖐	👇	☠	90
→	✈	🚩	⌘	❖	☹	40
48	38	72	55	70	65	50

↘	↓	↓	↓	↓	↓	↙
→	5	15	14	11	2	47
→	14	8	12	16	18	68
→	3	16	6	17	13	55
→	13	21	15	20	21	90
→	3	12	8	6	11	40
48	38	72	55	70	65	50

👎	=	2
✈	=	3
👍	=	5
❖	=	6
⌘	=	8
☹	=	11
🚩	=	12
☺	=	13
😐	=	14
🖐	=	15
💣	=	16
👉	=	17
☝	=	18
👇	=	20
☠	=	21

PUZZLE PREVIEW
NIGHTMARE BLOCKS

The 15 letters in **NIGHTMARE BLOCKS** have different numerical values. Place values to agree sum totals horizontally, vertically and diagonally.

N	=	
I	=	
G	=	15
H	=	21
T	=	
M	=	18
A	=	
R	=	
E	=	
B	=	
L	=	
O	=	
C	=	17
K	=	
S	=	13

↓ = ⌒ Enter values when worked out   Green boxes are "given" values

↘	↓	↓	↓	↓	↓	↙
→	A	H	B	L	R	73
→	G	S	K	H	T	74
→	O	E	G	E	T	49
→	B	M	I	C	M	83
→	N	I	N	R	A	55
82	60	68	72	75	59	47

↘	↓	↓	↓	↓	↓	↙
→						73
→		13		21		74
→			15			49
→		18		17		83
→						55
82	60	68	72	75	59	47

1
6
8
10
11
12
13
14
15
16
17
18
19
20
21

Solution Overleaf

© Les Page 2020 A preview of another Les Page title *Nightmare Blocks* - for details see page 3 or visit www.tarquingroup.com.

SOLUTION

↘	↓	↓	↓	↓	↓	↙
→	A	H	B	L	R	73
→	G	S	K	H	T	74
→	O	E	G	E	T	49
→	B	M	I	C	M	83
→	N	I	N	R	A	55
82	60	68	72	75	59	47

↘	↓	↓	↓	↓	↓	↙
→	1	21	20	19	12	73
→	15	13	11	21	14	74
→	8	6	15	6	14	49
→	20	18	10	17	18	83
→	16	10	16	12	1	55
82	60	68	72	75	59	47

A	=	1
E	=	6
O	=	8
I	=	10
K	=	11
R	=	12
S	=	13
T	=	14
G	=	15
N	=	16
C	=	17
M	=	18
L	=	19
B	=	20
H	=	21

Scribble Page

Need a New Tarquin Challenge?

We have a series of number and logic puzzles for a variety of ages and skill levels. See all at our website - but here are a selection:

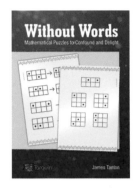

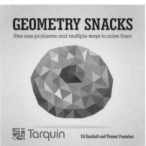

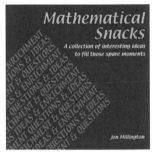

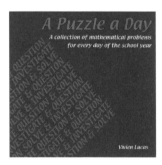

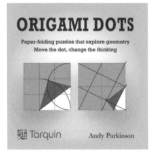

Bestselling titles like Without Words, Geometry Snacks and A Puzzle a Day will be joined by Birds, Bees and Burgers in 2021.

Buy Tarquin books in most trade outlets or from www.tarquingroup.com